W9-AFT-270

Spit Nests, Puke Power,

and Other Brilliant

Bird Adaptations

LAURA PERDEW

Illustrated by Katie Mazeika

Bird Limerick

There once was a hoatzin bird,

Whose burps were really absurd!

It never ate beans,

It only ate greens,

So foul, its nickname was "stinkbird."

Birds have many amazing and bizarre adaptations to help them survive. It's easy to see how herons' extra-long legs help them wade through water. And to hear how a woodpecker's sturdy beak can tap, tap, tap on trees to find food.

But do you know what swiftlets use to build their nests?

1

Spit!

It's true! Swiftlets dribble out long strands of gooey saliva to create their nests. When the spit dries, the cup-shaped nest is rock-hard.

This adaptation makes it easy to build nests high on cave or cliff walls to keep safe from predators.

Wouldn't it be awesome if you could build a fort out of your own spit?

It can take two months for swiftlets to build their nests.

Male bowerbirds build their own
kind of forts, called bowers.

Guess what they do next—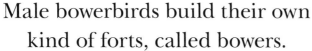

Bowerbirds use
colorful berries,
shells,
flowers,
and other objects to add the perfect touch.

These aren't nests, though. All that work and
it's not a nest? Nope. Males create bowers just
to show off how smart and fit they are.

After spending months building and decorating their bowers, the males spend even more time maintaining and defending them.

Birds do all kinds of crazy things to attract a mate, including a birdie boogie.

When it's time to find a partner, male birds-of-paradise aren't shy about showing off their dance moves and strutting their stuff.

These complex dances show the female

They will puff up, bobble, bob, bow, fluff, waggle, shimmy, and shake, hoping a female will pick them as a mate.

which males are the strongest and most well-adapted.

Blue-footed boobies do a mating dance, too. It's like the hokey pokey!

"Put your right foot in, put your right foot out, put your right foot in and shake it all about."

While males do the hokey-pokey, females check out their feet. Those large, webbed, blue feet are also for paddling through water and for keeping eggs warm.

Females look for a mate with the bluest feet.

The bluest feet tell her that a male is healthy and STRONG.

Emperor penguin dads use their feet to keep eggs warm, too. Their feet protect the eggs from the **super c-c-cold** Antarctic air.

Even after hatching, the young stay on a parent's feet, tucked under the feathers to stay snuggly warm.

But how do the adults stay warm?

They huddle!

They even take turns being in the middle, where it's warmest.

Now that's teamwork!

10

The male emperor penguins incubate the eggs while the mothers go off to eat. Females don't return until after the chicks have hatched.

Emus don't use their feet for incubating or impressing—they use theirs for running, jumping, and kicking.

They can run as fast as 30 miles per hour and can jump 7 feet in the air. Good thing, too, because they can't fly.

If running from trouble doesn't work, they defend themselves with a powerful kick.

Hi-ya!

In addition to running, jumping, and kicking, emus also use their powerful legs for swimming.

Many vultures are bald to keep bacteria and **blood** from sticking to their feathers when they eat a dead animal.

Do you know how vultures defend themselves?

Puke power!

Their stomach acid is strong enough to kill the deadly bacteria that lurk in the rotting, smelly, dead meat they eat for dinner.

When they're threatened, they puke, and if the smell doesn't send a predator running, the burning acid in the vomit will.

Never make a vulture mad!

Hoatzins have a strange digestive system, too.
It's a lot like the stomach of a cow.
Friendly bacteria in their gut help
break down the leaves they eat.
But instead of tooting a lot like cows do,

hoatzins burp!

Their burps are so smelly that hoatzins have
the nickname "stinkbird." They may be
stinky, but predators leave them alone.

16

Hoatzins are the only bird with this type of digestive system.

Shoebill storks' beaks are so powerful they can eat small crocodiles, lungfish, and snakes.

18

Shoebill storks are in good company when talking about bizarre bird adaptations. They poop on their own legs.

On purpose!

They do that to cool down.

Bet you can think of lots of other, more polite ways to cool off!

But these beasts of a bird can pretty much do whatever they want—they are the bosses of the swamp because of their huge, powerful (and frightening) beaks.

**Toco toucans have
big beaks, too.**

They use their beaks to help them cool off.
Heat escapes through the beak's thin outer layer.

They also use their beaks to pluck fruit from
trees or to dig out a hole in wood for a nest.

**Did you know they use their
beaks to play catch, too?**

During mating season, toucans play catch with fruit using their beaks.

Hummingbirds have an entirely different kind of beak.
Their beaks are long and thin, which
helps them reach inside flowers.

Then, their tongues work like small,
elastic pumps, moving so fast they lap up
nectar with as many as **20 licks per second**.

You'd be able to down a milkshake in no
time if you had a tongue like that.

No straw needed!

Hummingbirds can fly like helicopters—they hover and fly up, down, sideways, backwards, or upside down!

Owls are adapted for another kind of meal. And a lot of it has to do with their feathers. Because of their fluffy feathers, owls can fly almost silently and

hunt like ninjas.

Plus, the feathers on their faces collect and direct sound right to their ears. This helps owls to locate their prey.

Imagine having a face full of feathers that helped you find dinner!

Not only can the great horned owl fly almost silently, their wings are short and wide, which allows them to fly easily between trees in a forest.

Crows are
one of the smartest species
of birds on Earth.

While owls are thought of as wise, one of the smartest, craftiest birds is the American crow.

Crows can recognize faces and tell their buddies which kids are kind and which are not.

So remember, if you are nice to a crow, the crow will remember you. And if you are not nice to a crow, it will remember that, too.

Mean people get mobbed!

All birds have adaptations that help them survive wherever they live!

What other bizarre bird adaptations can you uncover?

Build Your Own Bird

Birds have beaks, wings, feathers, and interesting feet. Each of these features helps a bird to survive in its habitat.

Blue-footed booby

WHAT YOU NEED

paper, colored pencils or crayons

WHAT YOU DO

It's your turn to design a bird.
Where does your bird live—
the Arctic, jungle, desert, forest,
or near the water?
What does it eat?
Does it build a nest?
Think about what kinds of beak, wings, feathers,
and feet it needs to survive in that environment.

Now, draw your bird.
Keep in mind the different features it needs.
After you draw a picture of it, write about it.
Describe the habitat and your bird's special adaptations.
Maybe it even has a special song or call
to communicate.
Does it build a nest?
Don't forget to name your bird!

Emperor penguin

Glossary

Shoebill stork

adaptation: something about a plant or animal that helps it survive in its habitat.

bacteria: tiny living things found in animals, plants, soil, and water. Some bacteria are helpful and some are harmful.

bower: a kind of shelter.

colony: a population of plants or animals of one species that lives in a particular place.

digestive system: the body system that breaks down the food you eat.

environment: the area in which something lives.

habitat: an area that a plant or animal calls home.

incubate: to keep a developing egg warm.

mate: a partner.

Toco toucan

mating: reproducing to make something new, just like itself. To make babies.

nectar: a sweet fluid made by flowers that attracts insects.

predator: an animal that hunts another animal for food.

prey: an animal that is hunted and eaten by another animal.

saliva: the clear liquid in the mouth that helps you swallow and digest food.

species: a group of living things that are closely related and produce young.

Male bowerbird

stomach acid: a fluid in the stomach that breaks down food.

warm-blooded: describes animals that can keep themselves warm with their own body heat, such as humans, birds, and bears.

CHECK OUT THE OTHER TITLES IN THIS SET!

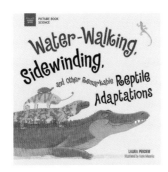

Nomad Press

A division of Nomad Communications

10 9 8 7 6 5 4 3 2 1

This book was manufactured by CGB Printers, North Mankato, Minnesota, United States
August 2020, Job #300937
ISBN Softcover: 978-1-61930-952-4
ISBN Hardcover: 978-1-61930-949-4

Educational Consultant, Marla Conn

Questions regarding the ordering of this book should be addressed to
Nomad Press
2456 Christian St., White River Junction, VT 05001
www.nomadpress.net

Printed in the United States.